stronger

I'll make it through the rainy days
I'll be the one who stands here longer than the rest
When my landscape changes, rearranges
I'll be stronger than I've ever been
No more stillness, more sunlight,
Everything's gonna be alright

I know that there's gonna be a change
Better find your way out of your fear
If you wanna come with me
Then that's the way it's gotta be
I'm all alone and finally
I'm getting stronger
You'll come to see
Just what I can be
I'm getting stronger

Sometimes I feel so down and out
Like emotion that's been captured in a maze
I had my ups and downs
Trials and tribulations,
I overcome it day by day,
Feeling good and almost powerful
A new me, that's what I'm looking for

Bridge
Chorus

I didn't know what I had to do
I just knew I was alone
People around me
But they didn't care
So I searched into my soul
I'm not the type of girl that will let them see her cry
It's not my style
I get by
See I'm gonna do this for me

Repeat chorus til fade

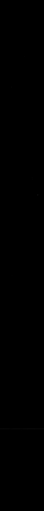

モヂジラミミヂ

WARNER BROS. PUBLICATIONS
Warner Music Group
An AOL Time Warner Company
USA: 15800 NW 48th Avenue, Miami, FL 33014

WARNER/CHAPPELL MUSIC	Carisch NUOVA CARISCH	IMP INTERNATIONAL MUSIC PUBLICATIONS LIMITED
CANADA: 15800 N.W. 48TH AVENUE MIAMI, FLORIDA 33014	**ITALY:** VIA CAMPANIA, 12 20098 S. GIULIANO MILANESE (MI)	**ENGLAND:** GRIFFIN HOUSE, 161 HAMMERSMITH ROAD, LONDON W6 8BS
SCANDINAVIA: P.O. BOX 533, VENDEVAGEN 85 B S-182 15, DANDERYD, SWEDEN	ZONA INDUSTRIALE SESTO ULTERIANO **SPAIN:** MAGALLANES, 25	**GERMANY:** MARSTALLSTR. 8, D-80539 MUNCHEN **DENMARK:** DANMUSIK, VOGNMAGERGADE 7
AUSTRALIA: P.O. BOX 353 3 TALAVERA ROAD, NORTH RYDE N.S.W. 2113	28015 MADRID **FRANCE:** CARISCH MUSICOM,	DK 1120 KOBENHAVNK
ASIA: THE PENINSULA OFFICE TOWER, 12th FLOOR 18 MIDDLE ROAD TSIM SHA TSUI, KOWLOON, HONG KONG	25, RUE D'HAUTEVILLE. 75010 PARIS	

Project Manager: Jeannette DeLisa
Book Art Layout: Ernesto Ebanks
Album Art: © 2001 Maverick / Warner Bros. Records Inc.

hotos: Regan Cameron, Patrick DeMarchelier, David LaChapelle, Jean Baptiste-Mondino,
Mark Romanek, Rankin, Peter Lindberg, Mario Testino, Frank Micelotta, Steven Meisel,
Gilles Bensimon, Rosie O'Donnell, Melody McDaniels, Herb Ritts
Album Art Direction: Kevin Reagan
Album Design: Kevin Reagan / Bret Healey

www.madonnamusic.com
Management: Caresse Henry / Caliente Management

CONTENTS

I would never dare attempt to delve into the psyche of a Madonna fan, however ardent, to try and examine the emotions that she impels upon them. And I am no expert in Madonna, or music, but I feel that having spent some time with her, in the capacity that I have, I am able to offer a distinctly different insight into Her Royal Highness, Madonna R., Queen of Pop. • • • I first met Madonna when I was a runner at SKA films, the production company owned by Guy Ritchie and Matthew Vaughn. During my first few days working there, her "Ray Of Light" video was on the TV and Guy discussed with me "how good" Madonna looked. That, I thought, would be the end of that. Little was I to know that Madonna would share the sentiments that Guy had bestowed upon her and three years later, treat them both to a son, Lourdes a brother and ultimately become Mrs. R. Good show! • • • I know very little of Madonna's background but after the aspiring ballerina's move from Michigan to New York in 1977, she firmly pulled up a chair at the pop music table. The chair soon became a throne. She then quickly found herself at the head of that table and sovereignty followed during the 80's. Madonna augmented her reign throughout the 90's, evolving at a rate that more than outweighed even her closest of rivals and with each evolution revolution, procured greater reverence and admiration.• • • I am writing this mid-shoot on "Love, Sex, Drugs & Money," Mr. Ritchie's latest film in which he has very kindly allowed his spouse to further her film career...by working in the catering truck. Without fail Madonna is on set every morning at 0500, hairnet on, cigarette in mouth, making tea and flipping eggs for the hungry crew. "She's not bad," said one of the burly electricians yesterday, "but she keeps burning the fucking bacon, it has to stop, or she has to go!" I witnessed the grip tossing his sandwich into a bin remarking, "I know she's the Guv'nor's wife and all but she should stick to what she does best." I asked Madonna about the bacon but she refused to comment.• • • Her music career has proven much more fruitful than her foray into the fry-up. But, as with her kitchen skills, it too has been tainted with controversy. "Erotica," quite possibly the rudest song of all time, featuring such shocking lyrics as "I'd like to put you in a trance," caused such disputations when it was released in 1992 that children were actually banned from listening to any music for over 7 months. As usual, it was the same bunch of over-sexed weirdos that unzipped their gimp masks and complained that if you listen carefully, Madonna is daring to sing a song about things that people do. What most people failed to realize, was that if you played it backwards at 33rpm, it actually told you to put all your clothes on and never talk to the opposite sex. Ever. • • • "Deeper and Deeper," from the same album, lowered some of the upturned noses caused by the "Erotica" single. But they were soon raised again when they discovered that the track was about a miner coming to terms with his homosexuality, "I can't help falling in love, I fall deeper and deeper the further I go," he sings as he disappears deep into the dark shaft.

The first chapter of the 1994 Bedtime Stories album was "Secret," a song that tackled the hard-hitting issue of transvestites. Documenting a man's sudden realization that his girlfriend is packing much more than she promised and as he/she shares his/her secret with him, she sings the crushing prose "…happiness lies in your own hand…" Think about it. Think harder. • • • With "Human Nature" Madonna really expressed herself with a defiantly unashamed dig at those that had dared to finger wag. People often discuss the strange behavior that people exhibit, supposedly provoked by Madonna, well let me tell you this: After watching a leather clad M spank her leather-clad Chihuahua in the accompanying video, my German Shepherd (who shall remain anonymous) gave me 'come to kennel eyes' for two days. At first I neglected his advances but I eventually succumbed to his demands and bought similar outfits for the both of us. This was a purchase that I was soon to regret. • • • "Bedtime Story" saw Madonna collaborating with Nellee Hooper and Björk. Unearthing trance-house music, they succeeded in adding their own ingredients and unleashing it upon a welcoming nation. After opening with a futuristic Barbarella-esque shot of Madonna, the video for "Bedtime Story" rapidly descends into an exquisitely executed nightmarish vision that would have had the Brothers Grimm giving it two fee-fi-fo-thumbs way, way up. • • • In 1995 the press would have us believe that Alan Parker received an 8-page letter from Madonna demanding that she should work on the catering truck on his upcoming film "Evita," but Parker refused. "I didn't even finish reading the letter," said the director, "I had heard about how she burnt the bacon on "Desperately Seeking Susan" and I didn't want her anywhere near our food." Down, but not out, Madonna wrote back to Parker saying that if he wasn't going to let her cater for the film, how about allowing her to play the lead? Parker agreed immediately. Not only did Madonna win a Golden Globe for her outstanding performance as Eva Peron, she made "Don't Cry For Me Argentina" her own. Most importantly, the crew did not go hungry. • • • Bittersweet was the order of the day for "The Power of Good-bye," a haunting song that defies the laws of physics. William Orbit, with whom she unites throughout her "Ray of Light" album, is blatantly unaware of Newton's Law, as he failed to spot this obvious mistake. Madonna claims that "…there's no greater power than the power of good-bye…" Is that right? Well, the power of good-bye may be effective when it comes to relationships, but it's not going to allow my portable DVD player to work, no matter how many times I bid it farewell. Electricity, gas, wind, water and of course nuclear are all much greater powers than the power of good-bye. Even steam is, it can move trains. • • • Physics aside, this album has become one of her most revered releases and found itself the recipient of four Grammys®. A little known fact, is that the ethereal track "Frozen" was originally commissioned by Haagen Dazs for a commercial, but its unearthly qualities were deemed unsuitable for ice-cream promotion. Madonna, although a little disappointed, kept her chin up and released it anyway. (Apparently Ben & Jerry also refused the track.)

The gap between her previous and latest albums was perfectly bridged by the track "Beautiful Stranger," recorded for the soundtrack of "Austin Powers The Spy Who Shagged Me". Well known for her thoughtless lyrics, Madonna reached new boundaries with these. After spending our lives being advised not to talk to strangers and telling our children the same, she not only talks to one, she falls in love with one—and sings to him. Think, woman. • • • And so to her latest album, "Music." "Don't Tell Me" is a dust-coated, rootin-tootin, thigh-slapper of a track. And although a great tune, Madonna displays irresponsible behavior once again, this time in the video. For starters, she walks down the middle of the road, narrowly avoiding being hit by a truck. Her lyrics also suggest that we "...Take the black off a crow." I tried this and the sight of a bald, pink crow hopping around my yard was enough to make me hate birds forever. Incidentally, John Wayne would revolve in his spitoon if he saw those 'manly' cowboys leaping about and line dancing as they do. Strangely, the video ends with Madonna riding a huge leather handbag. Must be symbolic (or belong to one of the cowboys.) • • • To find out exactly "What It Feels Like For A Girl," Guy told me that he followed her 'round one evening, with his DV Cam. Her nihilistic behavior that the footage shows, resulted in the video being censored and even banned on some networks. Madonna, ignoring her husband's pleas to calm down, is seen racing along busy streets in stolen cars. Her grandmother, an accessory to all this, is seated beside her, unflinching, as they ram into cars, motorbikes and even hockey players. To top it all off, Madonna squirts water into a cop's face and throws uneaten fries, yes uneaten, into a bin—damn her to hell. If you hadn't have banned that video we'd all have been at it. In fact, after seeing the video, I went out and stole this laptop upon which I write. And when I've finished, I'm going to smash it to pieces. • • • I am not a dancing man. I hate dancing. In nightclubs, I normally stand at the back of the room, calmly place both hands in my front pockets, tap my foot and, for a little variety, sometimes nod my head. Except for when I hear the title track from this album, which does exactly what it says on the tin. It "...makes the people come together..." but not in the way it probably intends. The "people come together" and stand and stare with gaping mouths as I unleash myself like a Tazmanian devil in front of them. When the song is over and the laughter has ceased, I slowly walk through the crowd, take my place at the back of the room and wonder who or what the bourgeoisie are. • • • So what next for Madonna? Over the past two decades she has proven herself a Diva, an Actress and an Icon. • • • She once told me that if her wealth and career were taken away from her, it wouldn't matter as she has everything she has ever wanted in her husband and children. You can't say fairer than that.

Successful Wife. Successful Mother. Terrible cook.

God Save The Queen(s)

Jan Cadan

DEEPER AND DEEPER

Words and Music by
MADONNA CICCONE, SHEP PETTIBONE
and TONY SHIMKIN

EROTICA

Words and Music by
MADONNA CICCONE, SHEP PETTIBONE
and TONY SHIMKIN

Moderately, with a heavy beat

N.C.

D/F♯   F♯m   D/F♯   F♯m

(Spoken:) Erotica…   Romance…

%% Verse:

D/F♯   F♯m   D/F♯

1. My name is Dita.   I'll be your mistress tonight.
2. Once you put your hand in the flame,   you'll never be the same.   There's a certain satisfaction
3. I don't think you know what pain is.

I'd

like to put_ you in_ a trance._
in a little bit of pain.
I don't think you've gone that way.

If I take you from behind, push myself into your mind when you
I can see you understand me, I can tell that you're the same.
I could bring you so much pleasure.

Omit 2nd time

least expect it,
If you are afraid, we'll raise above.

will you try to reject it?
I only hurt the ones I love.
I'll come to you when you say.

If I'm in charge and I treat you
I know you want me.

like a child,
I'm not gonna hurt you.

will you let yourself go wild, let my mouth go where it wants to?
I'm not gonna hurt you. Just close your eyes.

HUMAN NATURE

Words and Music by
MADONNA CICCONE, DAVE HALL, KEVIN McKENZIE,
SHAWN McKENZIE and MICHAEL DEERING

Moderate dance beat ♩ = 88

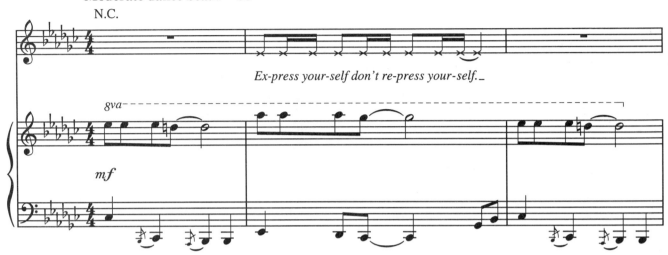

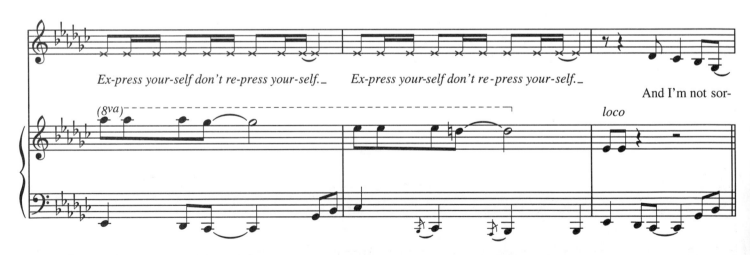

Human Nature - 7 - 1

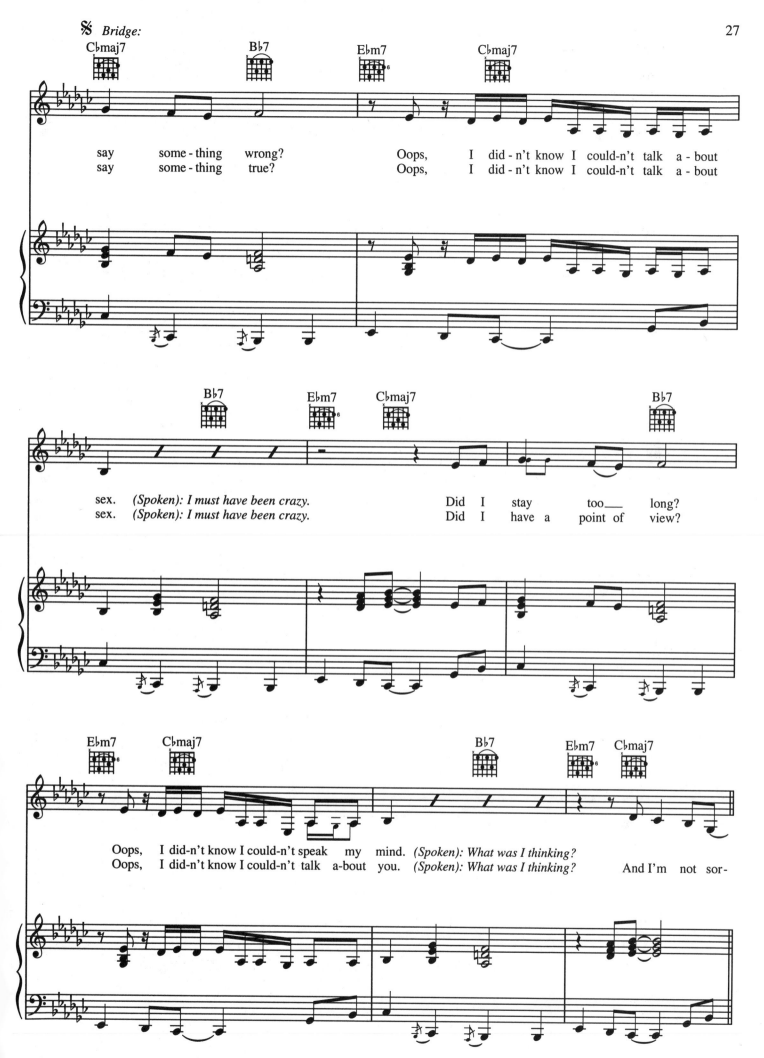

SECRET

Words and Music by
MADONNA CICCONE, DALLAS AUSTIN
and SHEP PETTIBONE

1. Things hav-en't been the same since you came____ in-to my life.____ You
2. You gave me back the par-a dise that I thought____ I lost for good.____ You
3. You knew all a-long what I nev-er want-ed to say.__ Un-

found a way____ to touch____ my____ soul____ and I'm nev-er ev-er, ev-er, gon-na
helped me find____ the rea-son____ why____ it took me by sur-prise that you
til I learned__ to love____ my-self,____ I was nev-er, ev-er lov-ing an-y-

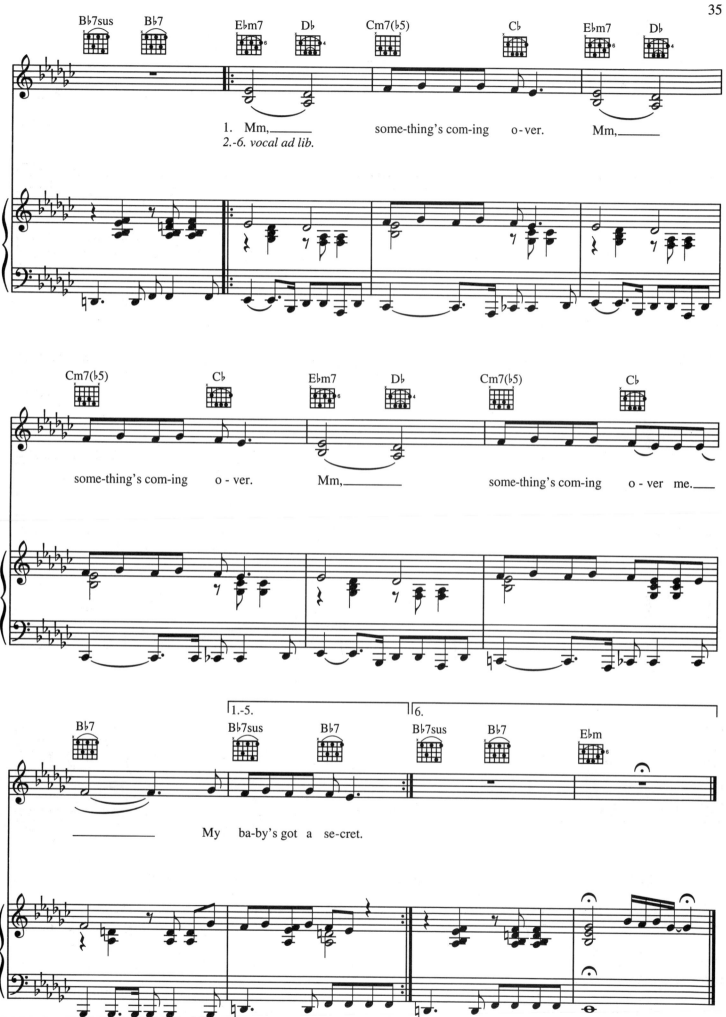

DON'T CRY FOR ME ARGENTINA

Words by
TIM RICE

Music by
ANDREW LLOYD WEBBER

* Original recording in key of B major.

Don't Cry for Me Argentina - 5 - 1

BEDTIME STORY

Moderately ♩ = 108

Verse 1:

Words and Music by
NELLEE HOOPER, BJÖRK GUDMUNSDOTTIR
and MARIUS DEVRIES

Bedtime Story - 6 - 1

44

ness. }
ness. }

Chorus:

Gm9

Let's get__ un - con - scious,__ hon - ey.

Let's get__ un - con - scious._____

Let's get__ un - con - scious,__ hon -

ey.

Let's get__ un - con - scious._____

D.S. 𝄋 al Coda   ⊕ Coda

THE POWER OF GOOD-BYE

Words and Music by
MADONNA CICCONE
and RICK NOWELS

The Power of Good-Bye - 7 - 1

48

Verse 3:
Your heart is not open, so I must go.
The spell has been broken, I loved you so.
You were my lesson I had to learn,
I was your fortress.

Chorus 2:
There's nothing left to lose.
There's no more heart to bruise.
There's no greater power than the power of good-bye.
(To Bridge:)

BEAUTIFUL STRANGER

Words and Music by
MADONNA CICCONE and WILLIAM ORBIT

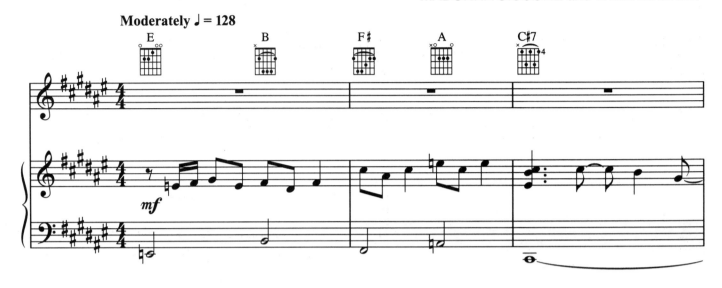

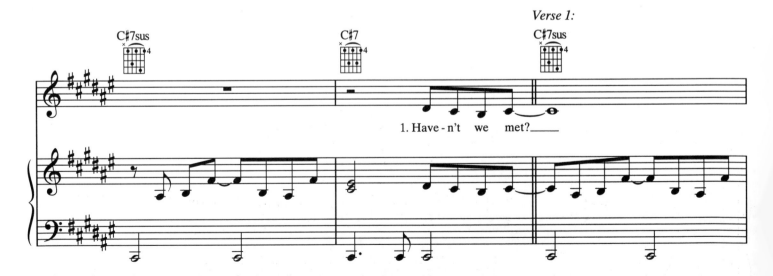

1. Have-n't we met?____

Verse 1:

FROZEN

Words and Music by
MADONNA CICCONE and
PATRICK LEONARD

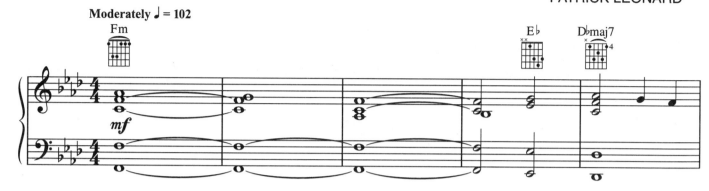

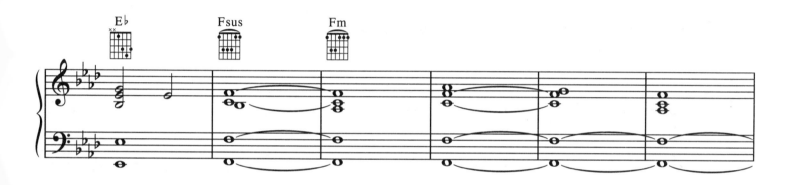

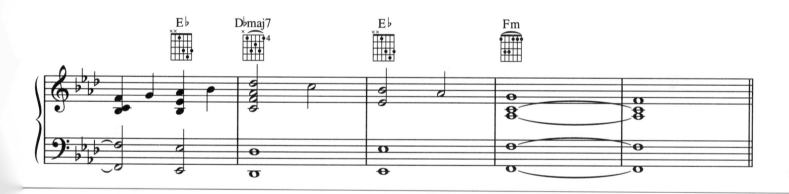

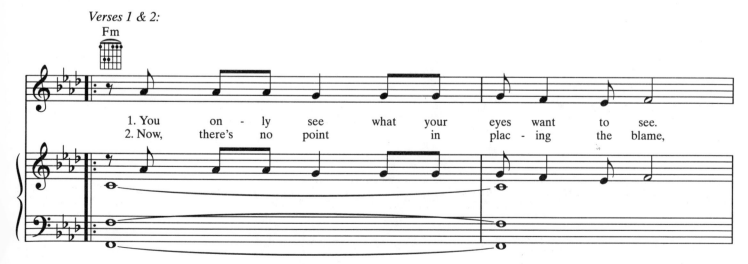

Verses 1 & 2:

1. You on - ly see what your eyes want to see.
2. Now, there's no point in plac - ing the blame,

Frozen - 5 - 1

How can life be what you want it to be?___ You're fro - zen
and you should know I suf - fer the same.___ If I should lose__ you,

when your heart's not o - pen.
my heart will be bro - ken.

%% *Verse 3:*

You're so con - sumed with how much you get.___
Love is a bird, she needs to fly.___
3. You on - ly see what your eyes want to see.___

You waste your time with hate and re - gret.___ You're bro - ken
Let all the hurt in - side of you die.___ You're fro - zen
How can life be what you want it to be?___ You're fro - zen

TAKE A BOW

Words and Music by
MADONNA CICCONE and BABYFACE

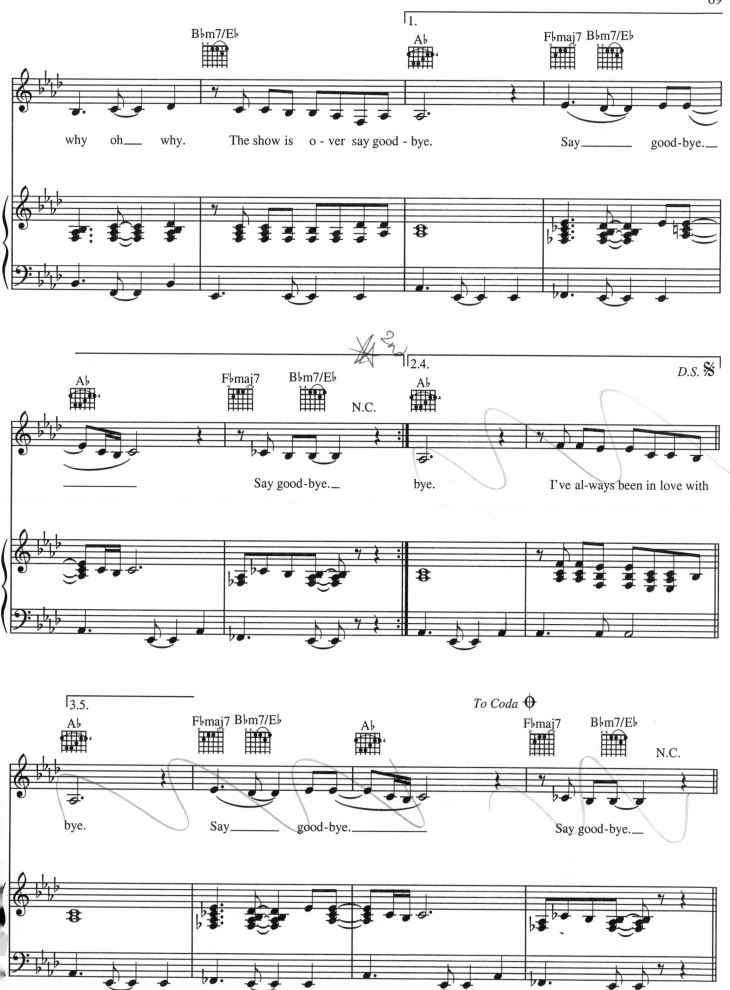

RAY OF LIGHT

Words and Music by
MADONNA CICCONE, WILLIAM ORBIT,
CHRISTINE LEACH, CLIVE MULDOON
and DAVE CURTIS

Ray of Light - 6 - 1

Verse 3:

3. Zeph-yr in the sky___ at night,___ I won - der___ do my tears___ of

mourn - ing___ sink be - neath___ the sun?___

She's got her-self a u - ni - verse___ gone quick - ly,___ for the call___ of

thun - der___ threat-ens ev - 'ry one.___ And I feel___

D.S. % al Coda

DON'T TELL ME

Words and Music by
MADONNA CICCONE, JOE HENRY
and MIRWAIS AHMADZAÏ

Moderately ♩ = 100

Verse:

1. Don't tell me to stop.___
2. *See additional lyrics*

Tell the rain not to drop,___   tell the wind not to blow_

Don't Tell Me - 5 - 1

Verse 2:
Tell me love isn't true,
It's just something that we do.
Tell me everything I'm not,
But please don't tell me to stop.
Tell the leaves not to turn
But don't ever tell me I'll learn.
Take the black off a crow,
But don't tell me I have to go.

WHAT IT FEELS LIKE FOR A GIRL

Words and Music by
MADONNA CICCONE
and GUY SIGSWORTH

What It Feels Like for a Girl - 6 - 1

84

What It Feels Like for a Girl - 6 - 6

DROWNED WORLD/ SUBSTITUTE FOR LOVE

Words and Music by
MADONNA CICCONE, DAVID COLLINS,
WILLIAM ORBIT, ROD McKUEN and ANITA KERR

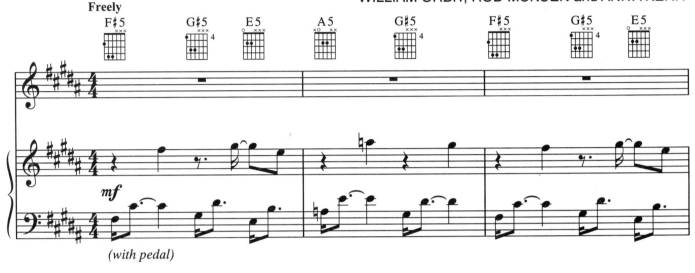

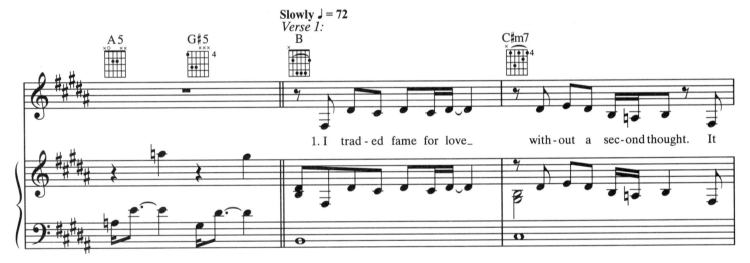

Drowned World/Substitute for Love - 5 - 1

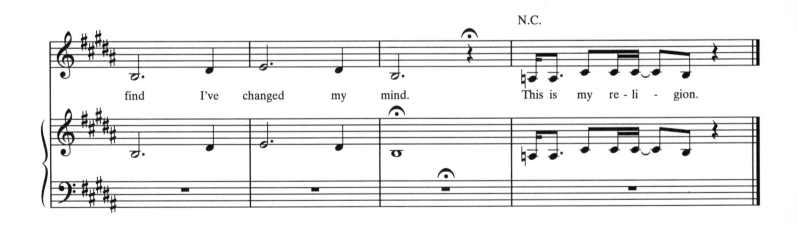

Verse 3:
Famous faces, far-off places, trinkets I can buy,
No handsome stranger, petty danger job that I can try.
No ferris wheel, no heart to steal, no laughter in the dark,
No one-night stand, no far-off land, no fire that I can spark.
(To Chorus:)

MUSIC

Words and Music by
MADONNA CICCONE and
MIRWAIS AHMADZAÏ

Moderately fast ♩ = 120

Do you like_ to boog-ie woog-ie? Do you like_ to boog-ie woog-ie?

Do you like_ to boog-ie woog-ie? Do you like_ my ac - id rock?_

Music - 4 - 1

Chorus:

Mu - sic__ makes the peo - ple__ come to - geth - er.__ (Nev-er gon-na stop.)

To Coda 1.

Mu - sic__ makes the bour - geoi - sie and the reb - el.__ (Nev-er gon-na stop.) 2. Don't

2.

(Nev-er gon - na stop.)

D.S. al Coda

Hey, Mis-ter D J. (Nev-er gon-na stop.)

⊕ *Coda*

(Nev-er gon-na stop.)

Do you like_ to boog-ie woog-ie? Do you like_ to boog-ie woog-ie?

Repeat ad lib. and fade

Do you like_ to boog-ie woog-ie? Do you like_ my ac - id rock?_

Verse 2:
Don't think of yesterday and I don't look at the clock.
I like to boogie woogie.
It's like riding on the wind and it never goes away,
Touches everything I'm in, got to have it every day.
(To Chorus:)